THIS BOOK BEL

Thank you for buying this book

Your satisfaction means a lot to us!
Please let us know how we are doing
by having us a review on Amazon

Your feedback really help us
Thank you !

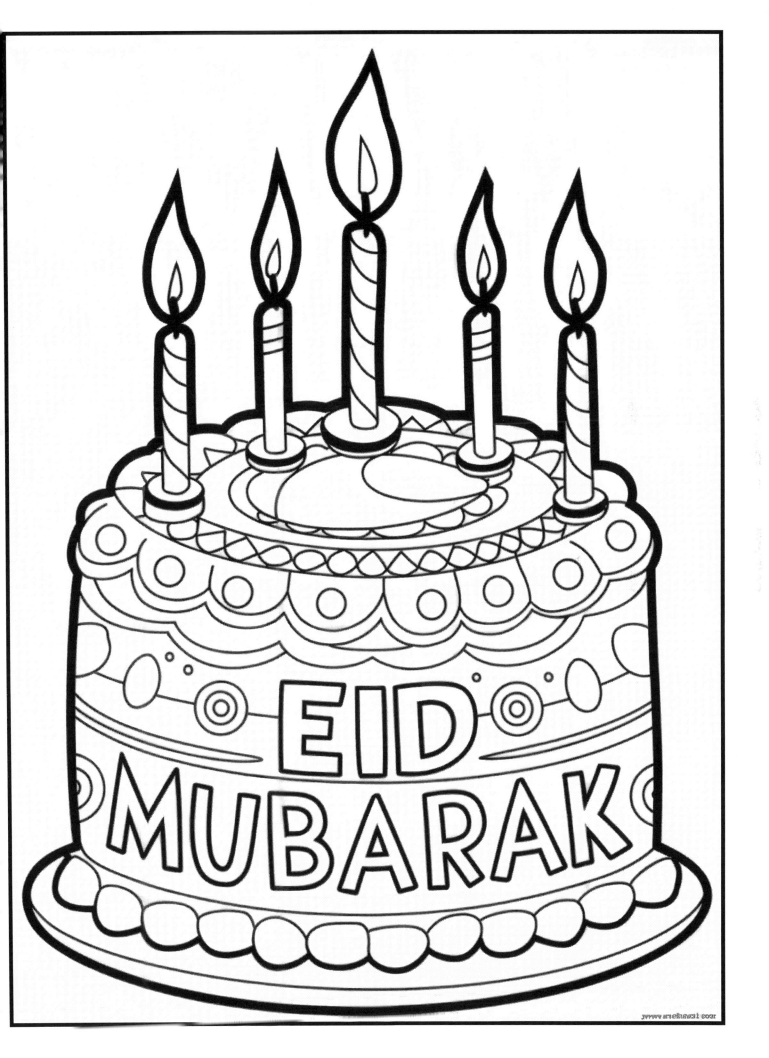

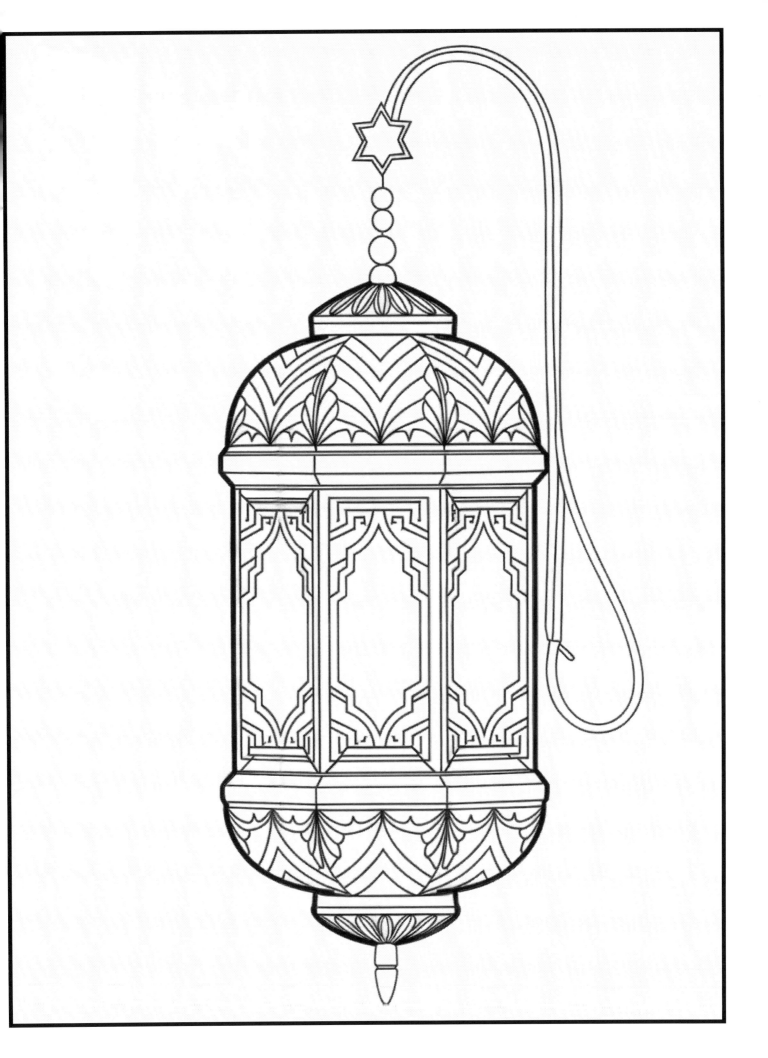

Made in the USA
Middletown, DE
03 June 2025

76490936R00057